CREATING AN EFFECTIVE
PARISH PASTORAL COUNCIL

CREATING AN EFFECTIVE PARISH PASTORAL COUNCIL

Robert G. Howes

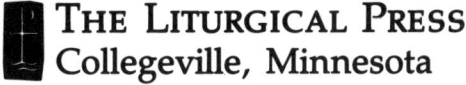

THE LITURGICAL PRESS
Collegeville, Minnesota

Cover design by Br. David Manahan, O.S.B.

Copyright © 1991 by The Order of St. Benedict, Inc., Collegeville, Minnesota. All rights reserved. No part of this book may be reproduced in any form or by any means, electronic or mechanical, including photocopying, recording, taping, or any retrieval system, without the written permission of The Liturgical Press, Collegeville, Minnesota 56321. Printed in the United States of America.

2 3 4 5 6 7 8 9

Library of Congress Cataloging-in-Publication Data

Howes, Robert G. (Robert Gerard), 1919–
   Creating an effective parish pastoral council / Robert G. Howes.
     p.   cm.
   Includes bibliographical references.
   ISBN 0-8146-1985-1
   1. Parish councils. 2. Catholic Church—Government. I. Title.
BX1920.H68   1991
254'.02—dc20

90-23941
CIP

CONTENTS

Preface		7
Models of Constellar/Choral Church		9
Chapter One:	Initial Insights	11
Chapter Two:	Our "Past is Prologue"	16
Chapter Three:	Lessons from "The Modern World"	21
Chapter Four:	Sharing/Planning	31
Chapter Five:	Evaluation	41
Chapter Six:	Procedure	49
Chapter Seven:	Pastoral Assembly/Task Forces	53
Chapter Eight:	Pastor and Council	57
Chapter Nine:	Check List for Your Parish Council	64
Chapter Ten:	Model Constitution and Bylaws	67
Glossary		73

PREFACE

This is a workbook. It is designed to help you think more insightfully about your parish council and, then, to activate your insights in effective impacts.

On the next two pages you will find two quick images of the ideal toward which the contemporary Church moves. All comparisons limp, but these images will suggest processes in which a good parish council will want to locate. And in which, indeed, it is summoned to play a very principal role. Bringing system (constellation) to random parishes (Milky Way) is surely a council accountability. Enabling an ever WIDER parochial WE (chorus) is surely also an accountability of a good parish council.

Toward the end of the text, you will find a model constitution and by laws for a parish council. It incarnates the ideas enunciated in the text. While, of course, subject to refinement in your local circumstances, it at least gives you something to reference as you establish your own norms.

At the end of the text there is a detailed glossary. This makes it easier for you. If you come across a term or terms which are not clear to you, go to these pages and clarify your understanding.

I wrote this text in the conviction that what Protestant pastor Bruce Blackie has called "static goodness" is no more acceptable in a parish council than it is in a pastor or a parishioner!

> A congregation that is unsure of what it is trying to leave behind and where it is going identifies no enemies to be dealt with and no mountain peaks to beckon it to higher orders of life. . . Static goodness stands in the way of growth.[1]

Each of us and all of us are summoned to "grow in grace and wisdom" as Christ himself did. My hope and prayer is that these pages will help you as you too go and grow.

[1] Bruce L. Blackie, *Gods of Goodness* (Philadelphia: Westminster Press, 1975) 43, 54.

A PARISH COUNCIL SHOULD BE
A constellation of related stars

in which persons, groups, processes and events relate systematically to one another.

Not a Milky Way:

in which persons, groups, processes and events sprawl centrifugally across a blur in space.

10 Models of Constellar/Choral Church

SINCE VATICAN COUNCIL II
WE CALL OURSELVES A PEOPLE OF GOD CHURCH

One way to image this is that we are involved in

A continual movement from a solo to a choral Church

Solo ———▶ Quartet ————▶ Chorus

1. In the solo Church of yesterday, Father sang in rectory and sanctuary mostly alone;
2. In the quartet (or sextet or octet) Church of today, Father sings with several ministers and councils;
3. In the choral Church we move toward, the whole parish sings with Father and the ministers and councils. There will still be solos and quartets. There must still be a conductor. And there is an urgency for commonwealth, i.e., for common lyrics and a common book. In the end there emerges a WIDER WE in which more and more people participate more and more effectively (performance + satisfaction).

As the Chinese adage puts its, "of a good emperor people say afterward, he did this and that. Of a superior emperor people say afterward, we did it all ourselves."

CHAPTER ONE
INITIAL INSIGHTS

Through each Christian individually and by parishes corporately living as saved, healed and reconciled people, we are credible signs of Christ's presence in the world.[1]

Christians are summoned to individual witness. Christians are likewise summoned, in the words of Vatican II, to partner continuously in "a common effort to attain fullness in unity."[2] There are many ways in which we incarnate this partnership. Among these, parish pastoral councils stand well forward. If parishes are where the ecclesial rubber meets the road, where theology becomes inspired and inspiring action, then their councils take on a primary importance in the maturation of each local people of God. This text focuses on that importance. It does so in a contemporary dimension and from the viewpoint of a professional pastoral planner with hands-on experience in thirty-one American and Canadian (arch)dioceses.

Pope Paul VI used a very apt analogy when he said that the boat which is the Church needs to *"navigare remis velisque"* (navigate with both oars and sails). Each Christian, each Christian partnership, requires what I call a present Pentecost. We can only succeed if the fiery winds of the Spirit inflate our canvas. But we require also strong shoulders rowing in unison at our oars. And we navigate best when we head for an agreed harbor with an agreed trip plan. If I focus in these pages rather more on the oars and the rowers, I mean in no way to deni-

12 *Initial Insights*

grate the Pentecost factor. Indeed, I propose that parishes which have been in one way or another "renewed" are enabled to row far better than parishes whose oars have not been enlightened in the Spirit. In these United States, many parishes have been or are being "renewed" in one way or another. Their canvas has been enthusiastically inflated. These pages respond to the question what next? How can parish pastoral councils enlarge and cohere a continuing partnership among those who row in and around them?

The task here is, through a dialogue of pertinent insights and impacts, to help you increase the effectiveness of your pastoral partnerships. *Effectiveness = Performance + Satisfaction.* We are effective when we work together only when a) we do more and more good things better and b) we feel more and more self-fulfilled in doing them. Parish pastoral councils, in close collaboration with their pastors, staffs, and other consultative groups, are effective in the same two dimensions.

Recently, one analyst of thirteen parish pastoral council guidelines across the nation wrote:

> Differences in understanding of councils—what they are, what they do, how they are led—are pronounced and widespread.[3]

Councils come in all shapes and sizes. Some work well, some do not. Some are big and complex, others small. In any normative text like this it is not possible to reflect each nuance. I can only speak in overall terms, relying on my readers to make such local adjustment as may be appropriate.

We are now well into the third decade since Vatican II. We've had many guidelines. There have been a number of workshops, pamphlets, many offices, and a few books. A National Pastoral Planning Conference started in 1973, an association of parish and diocesan councils people (PADICON) has existed since 1974.[4] The time has come when we should evaluate and build from our councils past. This, indeed, is why I have written this booklet!

We need first to develop contemporary *Insights*. What concepts and theories have been at work how? What can we learn from group dynamics, from organization development, from cybernetics, from planagement,[5] etc.? How should we now think and act as we unify and strengthen those who row our ecclesial oars? But we gather not to engage in empty academics, in some disembodied process. We need far more than pious theoretics, more than naked theology! We must also ponder *Impacts*. Some call it "the transfer factor." How can we get done effectively and with these people and these resources here, now and the day after tomorrow what our insights tell us? As we do this, we are immensely benefited by developments in the world around us. Writing in 1967, the very year when the first pastoral planning offices opened in Baltimore and Pittsburgh, one wise observer suggested:

> Perhaps God through the (Vatican II) Council has providentially allowed the Church to modernize its mission at the very point in time when the technical means exist for modernizing its method.

I like to propose that every American was born in Missouri! We're all *show-me-people*. If we convene and nothing happens afterward, if we brainstorm and there are no consequences, we are quickly turned off—and most of us will not reconvene. Thus impact in a generation which is massively prolific with the hardware and the software of how we best do things together must be of paramount concern in both pastoral planning and sharing.

This text looks initially at our councils past. It next surfaces some of the things I have learned as I review current experiences in planning and organization development. Subsequently, the focus shifts to the council/planning interface. Then, after foci on particular council dimensions, it moves to normative constitutional principles. I will repeat certain key points. Iteration and reiteration of such points is an essential ingredient in any effective learning process. Like a pile driver they stress again and again foundational elements in this process. I begin with three premises. The first is that we need to evaluate the track record of councils in the United States since Vatican II. If this cannot be done entirely, at least a quick analysis is possible and indispensable. The second premise is that there is minimal detail guidance for councils in the Council or in the Code of Canon Law. What does exist must be interpreted from a somewhat more but still substantially minimal treatment of diocesan pastoral councils. I regard both Council and Code as floors on which to build, not as ceilings restrictive of our prayerful creativity; they challenge us to put flesh on very bare bones. A third premise follows naturally from the absence of much official detail: while Pentecost and the Magisterium wind our sails, we must bring to bear on our oars the very best in human wisdom.

I am personally *a hard hat*. Hard hats are throughout concerned with outcomes. For instance, architects can discuss houseness at length, but unless and until they build a house here and now in this place for these people, architects starve. I recognize, of course, the en route importance of theory and of process. But I come out of a long background in the design arts and sciences. I'm concerned that when we share and plan in the Church something happens afterward. Indeed, I argue that the more effective councils become, i.e., the more they get things done, the better it is for all of us. It was surely no coincidence that many early proponents of MBO (management by objectives) came soon to evolve into proponents of MBO/R (management by objectives and results). Again, the show-me factor! This text, then, supplies both insight statements and impact suggestions.

Initial Insights 15

I have written a workbook, an action thesis. Some of my ideas will be controversial. There can be differences of opinion in so giant a subject area. There is simply no gospel from which we can derive absolute norms for our communal rowing! Still, once more from a design perspective, better to have made relatively tangible models than to flounder around in disembodied concepts, maybes, and perhapses. In any case, I succeed only if I help you grow a better council where you are. Meanwhile, I ask and promise union in prayer.

---

[1] Synod II, Diocese of Joliet, May 1989, 12.
[2] Dogmatic Constitution on the Church, Vatican II, 13.
[3] Mark F. Fischer, *Searching for the Mean in Parish Councils*, (Diocese of Oakland: 1988) 1.
[4] As of March, 1990, PADICON merged with the National Pastoral Planning Conference to become the Conference for Pastoral Planning and Council Development. Current CPPCD chair is Dr. Arthur X. Deegan, 891 Island Way, Clearwater, FL.
[5] This word emerged from "Planagement," a seminal text by Robert M. Randolph (American Management Association, 1975). Its thesis, to which I fully subscribe, proposes that planning and management are so intertwined that, rather than engaging in territorial warfare, it is preferable thus to speak of an indispensable commonality.
[6] Pat O'Meara in "America," June 10, 1967, 837.

CHAPTER TWO
Insight: OUR "PAST IS PROLOGUE"

It's now twenty-five years since Vatican II. We've had much experience with parish councils. While this text is not an academic study of that experience, it can surely be helpful to draw from it lessons which can guide us tomorrow.

Most early council guidelines were somewhat euphoric in regard to the conciliar parish, for example:

> The parish should be the training ground of apostles . . . a dynamic community . . . One important aspect of the current emphasis on co-responsibility within the Church is the sharing of the burden and privilege of setting goals and direction of efforts.[1]

Also:

> (A parish council is) a fraternity of Christians cooperating in the service and work of God; a collegial group which carries out the decisions it makes; a fraternity whose work is spiritual. It is not concerned only with buildings and finance, but with the formation of people in Christ, and the carrying out of Christ's mission in the world; a fraternity which seeks, with the priests and sisters, to coordinate and unify the apostolic work of the Church in the parish so as to make the Gospel known to all and all men holy.[2]

Perhaps such early hopes were too great. Indeed, one critic proposes that "we have grown recklessly unrealistic in our demands on our institutions."[3] In some dioceses, even, when

Our "Past Is Prologue" 17

councils had been widely established, that is, we had won the numbers game, there was little continuous support for them. Preaching high horizons, in many places there was inadequate notice, and funds, allotted to the process through which good councils were helped to mature. We seemed often to feel that we had merely to proclaim their existence and then let them go and grow on their own! Meanwhile deanery councils and diocesan councils, the big brothers, advocates, and models of parish councils, frequently floundered—and flounder. The net consequence was to cripple councils at all levels.

In any case, there have been successes, and I salute them. There have also been shortfalls. The first of these, again, was neglect, but there were others. A National Council of Catholic Men (1969) survey of one hundred fifty parish councils across America suggested four principal sources of council difficulty: lack of participation; we tried too much; dominance of the pastor; very little response or input from other parishioners. Among respondent comments were these:

- Overall indifference
- Our council died from frustration and lack of success in any real venture
- Lots of details move slowly but people expect too much too fast
- Our biggest problem is that we are full of ideas that cost money

An archdiocesan poll in Detroit (1970) identified "lay domination, clergy resistance and apathy" as major council problems. Surveying "diocesan advisory councils" in 1978, two observers pointed to widespread "powerlessness" and suggested:

> Yet, nevertheless, the vast majority (of respondents) feel the small amount of power they have been given presents no great problem. . . . (This) severe shortsightedness . . . magnifies

the almost fatal problem of powerlessness by adding the complications of complacency.[4]

A national survey of diocesan councils (1984) notes a) "concern and frustration with clergy support,"[5] and "tensions exist between DPCs and the clergy,"[6] and b) that "the relationships between the DPC and other diocesan agencies and bodies are not strong,"[7] and "the links between them are not as strong as they might be."[8] Among respondent comments were:

- Councils need publicity and visibility on a continuing basis
- A full-time, salaried staff person is needed for an effective council
- (We need to) work on clarifying relationships

While all of the above speak to diocesan councils, surely there are parallels in regard to parish councils.

Adding my own observations, I would identify these as the main problem areas which have fretted many parish councils:

1. *Apathy.* An unwillingness a) on the part of dioceses, b) on the part of many lay persons, and c) on the part of many priests to pitch in and help councils grow beyond disembodied "guidelines." This is not, in one sense, surprising. In national elections, however widely and insistently promoted, few Americans vote. Even fewer join active civic committees except when they become neighborhood veto groups. Likewise, if and as councils flounder largely inconsequential, parishioners quickly estimate membership in them as similarly inconsequential. Nor have we in most places provided opportunities, e.g., assemblies and task forces, for Catholics who cannot or will not accept membership on eternal committees. Clergy, meanwhile, remain not infrequently uncertain as to how their once solo role in parishes should now blend with others in a choral church. Many too are older and habituated to "one man parishes."

Our "Past Is Prologue" 19

To share responsibility gracefully with their parishioners is not easy for them. Dioceses, confronted with multiplying central bureaucracies and sometimes strapped for funds, tend often to regard council offices as "luxuries we cannot afford." Still and all, whatever its origins and excuses, apathy is a major source of council frustration.

2. *Relationships.* Here again the parable of the Milky Way versus the constellation! We have often rethought and reorganized the way we daily do things together in our dioceses and parishes, our operational subsystems. We have, in most cases, not done likewise with our consultative subsystems. As custodians and advocates for a principle of pastoral wholeness, parish councils often stand ambiguous in rampant and random local subsidiarity. Meanwhile, deprived of effective linkages with good deanery and diocesan councils, their ambiguity in an ecclesial Milky Way increases.

3. *Powerlessness/Complacency.* As has been indicated, too many councils for lack of real red meat on their agendas become anemic. At best, they feed on inconsequential porridge. They run from brush fire to brush fire. They have little impact on the daily life of their parishes. And many members are content with such insignificance! Obviously, effective pastoral planning can overcome this flaw. Some councils do plan; many do not.

4. *Growth Motivation/Passion.* Where there's a will, there's a way. If there is now a Second Spring for parish councils in the United States, I see few swallows! They are seldom challenged, poorly supported, poorly related. But no one seems much to care. Check ecclesial literature. There are culpably few articles, ferverinos, etc. on the subject of parish councils either in professional or popular publications! Clearly, whatever the past and whatever the difficulties, we

need new notice, applause, and the continual fertilizer of enthusiasm all around if these tender plants are to grow!

Perhaps this is too pessimistic. We do have councils. Some of them are excellent, many good. But any evaluation of yesterday is more helpful if, rather than accolading accomplishments, it surfaces problems and recommends solutions. This, in any case, is how I view "the past (as) prologue" in this text!

---

[1] Diocese of Camden, N.J., November 22, 1970, 2.
[2] *It's Your Parish* (Diocese of Youngstown: 1969).
[3] Daniel Yankelovich, *New Rules* (New York: Random House, 1981) 5.
[4] Richard Schoenherr and Eileen Simpson, *The Political Economy of Diocesan Advisory Councils* (Madison: University of Wisconsin Press, 1978) 98.
[5] *Building the Local Church* (United States Catholic Conference, 1984) 45.
[6] Ibid., 46.
[7] Ibid., 43.
[8] Ibid., 44.

CHAPTER THREE
Insight: LESSONS FROM "THE MODERN WORLD"

No parish is an organization, but each parish has an organization. As we reckon up the role of a parish council in leadership and ownership, we properly reflect on our learnings in these subject areas. We are not, of course, restricted by what critics and experts have discovered in regard to organizations elsewhere in our time. There is so much intangible, so much Spirit in our gatherings. Still, we can and should learn how we can become more organizationally effective, i.e., how we can perform better and how we can be more self-satisfied, fulfilled in the process. Call it mission, call it pastoral planning, call it what you will. One conclusion is, in my view, inescapable. Undergirding Christ's contemporary presence in and through us deserves the very best wisdoms we can gather from "the modern world." Here are some of the lessons I have learned over the years. Hopefully, they can help you.

Marcus Aurelius centuries ago wrote:

> We are made for cooperation like feet, like hands, like eyelids, like the rows of upper and lower teeth . . . Things are somehow implicated with one another.[1]

It has long since been evident to us city and regional planners that as cities sprawled our farther and farther, civic centrifugalism must be complemented by new patterns in commonwealth.

22 Lessons from "The Modern World"

DECENTER AND REINTEGRATE, as Frank Lloyd Wright used to say, became our challenge. As we entered the 1980s, this urgency had multiplied in an increasingly centrifugal and broad-based dimension:

> The leaders of tomorrow may well have to deal with a far more decentralized and participatory society.[2]

"Today we live in a world of overlapping networks."[3] In our parishes too we deal more and more not with a monolithic structure but rather with "a network of linked groups."[4] And "our religion is primarily a matter of relationships."[5] It is, thus, not coincidental that we now speak of priests as "enablers of ministry." And yet, as we spin off more and more pastoral specialists, both staff and board, the dangers of shattering our wholeness in centrifugal excursions grows. "Tunnel vision is always the degenerative disease of specialists."[6]

LESSON #1

> *Confronted by a great deal of decentering, parish councils must be vehicles for the continual reintegration of their parishes.*

The parish council is, inescapably, an *intervenor* in the inertia of its parish. It proposes thoughtful and deliberate intervention in parochial "static goodness." But the practice of the intervenor is neither easy nor simple. Two decades ago, an expert critic wrote:

> The role of the intervenor in our society is about where the role of the medical doctor was in the early 1700s.

He added:

> (The role and path of the intervenor is) long and painful, confusing, difficult and frustrating. The trip, although exciting, fun-

damental and essential is difficult, exhausting and frustrating . . . there are no pat answers.[8]

As they assume this role and take this path, then, councils have both a right to and a continual need for help. Inertia is so comfortable. As Willa Cather put it, "man is the only animal that fights to stay in a rut!" True, as Gilbert Keith Chesterton once noted, "real development is not leaving things behind as on a road, but drawing life from them as from a root."[9] A wise council is no iconoclast. It intervenes not to destroy the past in a wild spasm of innovation. It intervenes to help its parish do good things better. Still and all, there is always a difficult element of change involved, and there will be resistance however carefully it incorporates the best of yesterday in its approach to the parochial tomorrow.

LESSON #2

Parish councils should never simply be spun off and then left to fend for themselves.

There is a continual need for resourcing councils, alike in skills and theology, as they intervene in parochial inertias. Each council should be able to avail itself of specific help from a specific and capable place and person(s) at diocesan headquarters.

All organizations must deal with subjective perceptions as well as with objective reality. It has been noted:

> An individual's reaction to any situation is always a function not of the absolute character of the intervention but of his perception of it. It is how he sees things that counts, not objective reality.[10]

Put another way, the feel becomes the real. Parish councils must reckon with widely diverse perceptions and theologies.

24 Lessons from "The Modern World"

Speaking of diocesan advisory groups, but surely applicable also to parochial groups, one recent critic suggests:

> Their members are heterogeneous . . . They are unsophisticated theologically and they are uninformed on many of the topics they discuss. On the other hand, they do reflect the church which is not a homogeneous group of experts.[11]

As a council moves forward, then, it must be equally concerned with attitudes as with structure, process, and papers. True, it cannot alone reorient the psyche of the parishioners it serves. But it must be a prime agent for this. Archaic, regressive thought patterns must be broken up before intervention can succeed. In short:

> Men cannot implant a new way of believing by willing it. To will it is a necessary but not a sufficient step. They must unfreeze their old and learn new behavior and attitudes.[12]

One way to engage a parish in a constructive ideology for its group tomorrow is through what has come to be known as "idealized design." The council develops a scenario for the parochial future. This is exciting, comprehensive, and reasonably possible. The principal advocate of such a method says:

> The selection of ideals lies at the very core of interactive planning . . . It facilitates participation in the planning process . . . (It) stimulates creativity and focuses it on organizational and individual development.[12]

Utopias are rare in our day. Few if any propose that we shall be drastically better tomorrow than we were yesterday or are today. Still, it is possible and wise to develop plausible scenarios as to how this parish can be ten years from now and then to yeast such scenarios through the parish as a whole. Napoleon said once that his armies succeeded because every soldier in them carried a field marshall's baton in his knapsack. It is only as the corporate visions of its pastor and council are shared with and digested by the persons in its pews that any parish can truly and consistenly "grow in grace and wisdom."

LESSON #3

Parish councils need to inform and motivate as well as proclaim. A good way to do this effectively is through the development and dialogue to consensus of scenarios for the parochial day after tomorrow. "Ownership (is) an essential element in motivation."[14]

It is often contended that planning is research and process, and I agree both are essential ingredients. General Eisenhower, indeed, is reputed to have said that plans are nothing, planning is everything. But this is only a half truth; more is involved. Planning is also outcomes. In fact, "planning and doing are parts of the same job. They are not separate jobs."[15] A recent critic has coined the expression "the Rain Dance" Syndrome.[16] He says it widely afflicts American planning. He draws the analogy of an Indian rain dance. The dancers, he suggests, are often far more concerned with the choreography and the subsequent tourist dollars than they are with whether it rains afterward! Not infrequently I have observed church "planning" in which everything is process and there are no outcomes and, indeed, little apparent concern that something happens afterward. While this kind of group dynamics may be interesting, it cuts no ice. And it turns off the movers and the shakers who may have entered the process anticipating results. They will not soon return if nothing occurs after that process. I admit it is not easy always to trace activities back to planning beforehand. Still, in my view, the so-called transfer factor, how what we plan can get done with these people and these resources in this place soon, must be an integral factor in all pastoral planning from the start. "Never a promise without a plan!"[17] "Every parish should both plan and follow through with plans."[18] The paper plan has to be brought to life.

LESSON #4

Councils should wear hard hats when they plan.

Councils must never rest content with mere Process. They must always be concerned that something get built and done here and now as a consequence of their planning.

Ralph Waldo Emerson proposed that "nothing great was ever achieved without enthusiasm."[19] Indeed, the word enthusiasm itself comes from two Greek words: *en* (in) and *theou* (god). Certainly, every parish council must be in-godded. "The objective," said one critic, "is to strike some sparks."[20] He added, "you have to have a vision and you have to care passionately."[21] A few years ago, a national commission warned that "we live among determined, well-educated and strongly motivated competitors."[22] To succeed, we must environ our cause with compelling conviction. More recently Lonnie Shealey, President of Lone Star Builders, suggested:

> Whatever we call it—enthusiasm, motivation, ambition, drive, desire or energy—it's a quality which plays a major role in success.[23]

And yet, almost a decade ago, one knowledgeable observer of the American scene pointed to "a strong increase in aimlessness and in hedonism."[24] A later critic proposed that:

> Spiritual entropy or an evaporation of the soul's boiling blood is taking place.[24]

Another critic speaks of us as "cynical Americans," widely distrustful of our institutions. "The moral influence of all religions," he suggests, "has declined,"[26] He goes on to call for managerial passion:

Management has entered an era of evangelism . . . Only passionate leaders and excellent companies will survive.[27]

And yet still another critic finds a dispassionate, don't rock the boat attitude prevalent in most "managers."

> The most notable characteristic of the managers and interviewees was their mannerly lack of intensity . . . (They were by and large) passionless.[28]

Reality thus seems to be impeding the ideal gospel preached in so much contemporary "planagement" literature!

In any case, fighting great odds in an at best corrosively indifferent world, lukewarmness in a parish council is inexcusable.

LESSON #5

While utopias soon are most unlikely in either Church or state, parish councils must be convicted and convinced, radiating a massive enthusiasm through the parishes and communities they serve.

To be a leader today is a difficult task. Indeed, many shy away from it. And yet, "the pastor who raises up leaders is best."[29] So is that council best which models for, encourages, and applauds parochial leaders! Excellent pastors and councils like excellent companies are always "nurturing champions and creating heroes."[30] "Strategic planning" under our steeples as well as in business and civic headquarters "must be completely geared to a strategic vision."[31] And such vision is far more effective when it is witnessed rather than merely taught. The modern world is, indeed, surfeited with talk, perhaps even with "pastoral letters." Examples, heroic lives, Christian champions—this in an age of anxiety and discontinuity is how vision best succeeds. Admittedly, it was much easier and simpler for priests to sing radiance solo in yesterday's Church. But today, again, we seek an ever WIDER WE, a truly choral Church. Leadership is thus now plural. It remains indispensable, and the council plays a very central role.

LESSON #6

Both in what they do and what they are, and in the visions they lift up and share, parish councils are summoned to the continuous practice and enablement of choral leadership in a people of God Church.

There are other lessons, surely. The point is to keep our ecclesial eyes and ears open. I often invoke the parable of the stamp collector. A collector examines every envelope which crosses his or her desk to see if the stamp on it may be of interest or of value. Non-collectors simply toss used envelopes away. I believe we in the Church today should be stamp collectors looking very carefully at every envelope from "the modern world" which crosses our desks for learnings which may be relevant in our maturation as an effective people of God.

True, neither pastors nor councils can shoulder the entire or even, perhaps, the primary burden of changing our times. Still, if incapable of candelabras, they are summoned to light local candles. There are many ways to phrase the challenge before the Church as we near a new century. In my view, one of the best statements of our global accountability was enunciated by Joe B. Wyatt, as, on February 24, 1983, he was installed as the Chancellor of Vanderbilt University in Nashville, Tennessee.

> (We have a) fundamental responsibility to understand change, to uncover indicators, to look for trades, to question assumptions, to dream better ways, to talk, to listen and to connect

Lessons from "The Modern World" 29

our philosophical, our ethical and our cultural heritage with the science and technology that is pushing us forward.[32]

If this is true of a brilliant academic, how much the more it applies to those who gather under steeples in an Age of Anxiety. Again, no pastor and no council can do it all. But we can and must begin. "Politics," someone once suggested, "begins in the precinct." So too religion begins in the parish!

---

[1] Marcus Aurelius, *Meditations II*, 1.
[2] Alvin Toffler, *The Third Wave* (New York: Morrow, 1980) 404.
[3] John Naisbett, *Megatrends* (New York: Warner, 1982) 205.
[4] Leo B. Waynich, Jr. (to the National Pastoral Planning Convention, San Antonio, Tex., February 15, 1979).
[5] John Dreher (Diocese of Providence, 1979).
[6] Peter Drucker, *The New Realities* (New York: Harper and Row, 1989) 84.
[7] Chris Argyris, *Management and Organization Development* (New York: McGraw Hill, 1971) 176.
[8] Ibid., 182, xiii.
[9] Cited in Knille, *As I Was Saying* (Grand Rapids, Mich.: Eerdmans, 1985) 267.
[10] Rensis Likert, cited in Irwin and Webber, *Management* (Homewood, Ill.: 1975) 179.
[11] Thomas Reese, *Archbishop* (New York: Harper and Row, 1989) 123.
[12] Argyris, *Management and Organization Development*, 192.
[13] Russell Ackoff, *Creating the Corporate Future* (New York: Wiley, 1981) 105, 116, 149.
[14] Lawrence W. Miller, *American Spirit* (New York: Morrow, 1984) 75.
[15] Cited in Steiner, *Strategic Planning* (New York: Free Press, 1979) 179.
[16] Ackoff, *Creating the Corporate Future*, ix.
[17] Zig Ziglar, *Top Performance* (Old Tappan, N.J.: Revell, 1986) 88.
[18] George M. Williams, *Improving Parish Management* (Mystic, Conn.: XXIII Publications, 1983) 16.
[19] *Circles* (1840) in *Selections from Ralph Waldo Emerson*, ed. Stephen E. Wickes (Boston: Houghton-Mifflin, 1957) 178.
[20] Tom Peters, *Thriving on Chaos* (New York: Knopf, 1987) 222.

[21] Peters and Austin, *Passion for Excellence* (New York: Random House, 1985) 288.
[22] National Commission on Excellence in Education, "A Nation at Risk," *New York Times* (April 27, 1983) 13.
[23] Cited in Ziglar, *Top Performance*, 207.
[24] Yankelovich, *New Rules*, 92.
[25] Allan Bloom, *Closing of the American Mind* (New York: Simon and Schuster, 1987) 51.
[26] Donald L. Kanter, *The Cynical Americans* (San Francisco: Jossey Bass, 1989) 6.
[27] Ibid., 130.
[28] Diane R. Margolis, *The Managers* (New York: Morrow, 1979) 36, 131.
[29] Williams, *Improving Parish Management*, 78.
[30] Peters and Austin, *Passion for Excellence*, 189.
[31] Naisbett, *Megatrends*, 94.
[32] *Vanderbilt Register*, February 25, 1983, 5.

CHAPTER FOUR
SHARING/PLANNING:
Two Sides of the Same Pastoral Coin

I. INSIGHT

Pastoral planning means goal setting and a new sense of responsibility to each other as a community of faith, grace and service. . . . It is shared responsibility at its very best.[1]

I don't know how you can do shared responsibility without some sense of goal setting.[2]

The Church in its "human condition" is not exempt from a primary "planagement" principle. The more people are involved as active partners in the process through which decisions are reached that affect them, the more they are likely to do those decisions. Indeed:

> (People) will no longer accept decisions handed down to them and will show their frustration by aggressively opposing the decisions or ignoring them.[3]

Another fundamental "planagement" principle proposes that systematic approaches to tomorrow are preferable to putting out brush fires, i.e., drifting from crisis to crisis. "The future by design rather than by chance" is how this is often said. Admittedly, we can never absolutely populate our tomorrows as we prefer, but we can move into them with collective forethought. In short, planning ahead!

The documentation on parish councils is, again, minimal. Even so, it is possible to assume from likewise minimal documentation on diocesan councils that they too are summoned to propose, dialogue, and evaluate: to plan. As microcosms of the parishes they serve, as pastoral generalists, parish councils too are planning as well as "prayer" committees. Through them, the local people of God estimates its mission, its resources, its purposes, and its thrust. It does this as an ever WIDER WE, thus assuring participation in decisions which affect the entire parish and making those decisions in a comprehensive context.

Indeed, a parish council which is not simultaneously planning is itself flawed. One critic describes the random parish thus:

> All too often there is no blueprint, no road map, no battle plan; there is no way authentically to evaluate what we are trying to accomplish as a whole, because there is no view of the whole at all. A great many new programs or activities are proliferated because they seem like good things to do. But why?[4]

The net result is a seriously dysfunctional chaos:

> When we lose a vision of the whole, and yet retain a commitment to the parts, we are in the midst of a stampede. Activities multiply with amazing quickness. We become locked into roles . . . Often we find ourselves afflicted with the do-ism syndome.[5]

If, indeed, we move into an increasingly choral Church in which more and more of us are summoned to "leadership," then a planless parish is like a chorus with no common book and no common lyrics! Voices rise spasmodically. There is no commonwealth of song. Its council is caught in a cacophony of dissonant singers. It spends its time helter skelter, trying to make some sense of the several noises. Again, to mix metaphors, a Milky Way, not a constellation!

At this point, a further brief excursion into what I mean by planning. There is neither need nor place for a massive trip. Simply, so that this fundamental partner in shared responsibility can be better understood, I will use just a few words. First of all, when Church people speak of pastoral planning, they enunciate an umbrella term. Pastoral planning encompasses management, organization development, cybernetics, etc. More specifically, planning is "essentially two processes—the defining of goals and the design of the programs."[6] To plan is:

> to formulate and execute a system of coordinated policies framed to have the effect of bending the foreseen trends toward realizing our ideals spelled out in advance as definite goals.[7]

In "To Teach as Jesus Did," the National Conference of Catholic Bishops used these words:

> Needs must be clearly identified, goals and objectives must be established which are simultaneously realistic and creative; programs consistent with these needs and objectives must be designed carefully, conducted efficiently and evaluated honestly.[8]

In my own view, *planning is coherence plus energizing projection.* It's a process which brings together things that belong together—like past, present, and future; like resources and targets; like advisors and doers. It projects the tomorrow we seemingly drift toward and the tomorrows we prefer. It energizes all of us, e.g., through vision, structural reform, etc., so that we can indeed reach that collectively preferred future. Planning is, further, basically polygamous. I defined it once as a mongrel sitting in a delta. It draws on many arts and sciences. It can be a stranger to none. It must be a prisoner of none. My students once asked Morton Hoppenfeld, planner for Columbia New Town, Maryland, if he was interested in this or that facet of urbanology, e.g., economics, art, highways.

He replied: "I'm interested in everything because, you see, I'm building a city." So too the planner is perhaps the most generalist of all professionals! To put it graphically, planners operate continually within a kind of matrix:

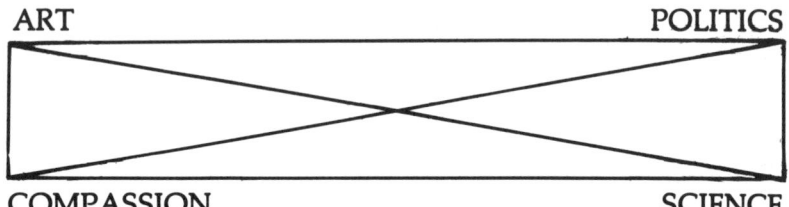

The good pastoral planner works in the vortex of all the elements which impact on the Church he or she serves. He or she can never, for example, overlook facilities or "community" or "worship space" or dollars and sense, etc. He or she must accommodate both the view from the pulpit and the view from the pew.

But planning is no static discipline. Years ago, some of us planners thought that all we had to do was proclaim a "master plan" and it would happen. Some of us too tended to look down on "mere mortals," convinced that they lacked our wisdom and had to be planned for rather than with. And we developed Year 2000 plans by the dozens! Meanwhile in the Soviet Union, it became soon evident that even the most erudite "Five Year Plans" very often collapse in Real Politik. In the same period, the pace of change and ambiguity so increased that we had to pull back from our initial conviction that tomorrow could, indeed, be designed in full and glorious detail. As one wise critic put it, when the fog level rises and intensifies around us, we must learn how to shorten our horizons and diminish our speed! We planners inherited from the Big Plans of Daniel Burnham and others at the turn of the century a dislike for little plans and muddling through. They seemed unworthy of our grand schemes for a much better civic tomorrow. They had nothing in them to stir people's blood. Since then, we have learned that step-by-step planning, however undramatic, is both inevitable and more effecitve. Today we acknowledge the inevitability of many little plans, much "incrementalism," and the need for political patience. I mean in no way to diminish the urgency for planning. I do suggest that we are dealing here not with the paramount and imperative kind of planning and management which some of us practiced yesterday but, rather, with a multi-faceted discipline which, like the world it serves, has changed. Perhaps most of all, the contemporary pastoral planner is keenly aware that he or she must involve and commit people or fail!

II. IMPACT

If, then, planning and councils are two sides of the same pastoral coin, how does a council plan? Suffice it here simply to a) summarize the three basic steps in an effective (performance + satisfaction) parish planning process and b) provide a quick graphic which you may choose to use as you publicize this process. For further detail see my The Liturgical Press leaflet (1989) "What Makes a Christian Parish?". Also my "How To Grow A Better Parish" packet (1986) published by Alba House.

Parish Planning—Three Steps

REDISCOVERY: Here a parish rediscovers itself currently and comprehensively. This involves:

    A. Responding collectively to the question—what makes a spiritually successful contemporary American parish?

    B. Gathering *objective* data about itself, e.g., demography, finances, school and CCD enrollment, the track record of its "councils."

C. Gathering *subjective* data about itself, i.e., how, polled on a saturation weekend, parishioners experience and feel in three categories: i) the strengths of our parish; ii) how our parish should improve; and iii) specifically about parish activities and groups such as sermons, outreach, the parochial council, youth ministry, etc. (Parish leaders should be polled separately. This can be done either by asking each of them to write L at the top of the survey form at the saturation, All-Masses polling, or by asking them to convene and complete the forms at another time. If the latter, obviously they should not submit forms at the saturation polling. The purpose of this is to give you a "control group," i.e., leadership survey results which can then be compared with pew results. Already, an important dynamic in your parish pastoral planning process!)
D. Gathering *contextual* data about itself, the ecology of the parish as a benefiting and contributing member of two larger communities: one ecclesial, the other civil.

ENGAGEMENT: Here parochial leaders gather, review the data from step #1 and *draft* i) a mission statement, ii) goals, and iii) objectives which then constitute the first refined but still raw materials for dialogue in step #3.

COMMITMENT: Here the parish as a whole, at a series of widely promoted open meetings, dialogues the data from step #1 and the *draft* proposals from step #2. Ultimately, a mission statement, goals (three year targets) and objectives (one year targets within each goal) are consensused and recommended as core items in an effective parish pastoral plan.

To navigate the boat that is our church with both oars and sails. (Paul VI) The fiery wind of the Holy Spirit as a local Pentecost again and again in our canvas, but also our best muscles stroking in unison at our oars!

"A common effort to attain fullness in unity."
(Vatican II, "Church," 13)

THE PURSUIT OF PARISH EXCELLENCE*—AN ITINERARY

⌈ IDEAL PARISH: USA TODAY** ⌉
  REDISCOVERY:
  how we are, feel and partner
⌊ OUR MISSION STATEMENT** ⌋

Why we exist here and now
as a community of faith, grace, and service.
↓
ENGAGEMENT:

Our pastoral leaders meet, dialogue and propose:
a. draft goals (three years) and objectives (one year)
b. draft strategies for accomplishing them.
↓
COMMITMENT:

As an ever WIDER WE, we gather, review all of above
and consensus our pastoral:
a. mission b. goals c. objectives d. responsibilities
e. strategies f. evaluation/update process, etc.
↓

| ROADMAP TO EXCELLENCE* IN OUR PARISH** |

As an ever WIDER WE, we write, commission, and commit
ourselves to our dynamic, living pastoral plan!

*Excellence means increasing our effectiveness.
Effectiveness = performance + satisfaction.
**Spiritual discernment is necessary throughout.
Unless He plans with us, we plan in vain!

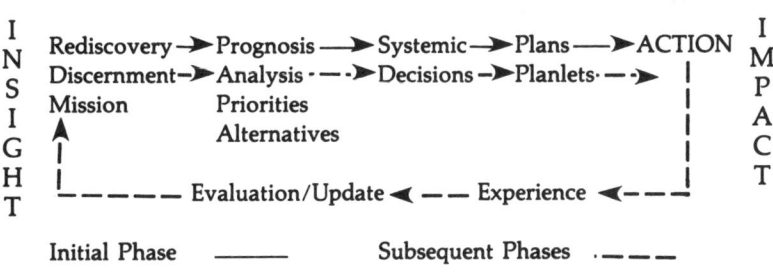

Initial Phase ———   Subsequent Phases . — — —

38 Sharing/Planning

Certain Particular Elements in Parish Pastoral Planning

1. SPIRITUALLY SUCCESSFUL PARISH (see *REDISCOVERY, A*)

    At this point, before you go local, you develop what may be described as an "idealized design" of the kind of parish parishioners prefer. This is neither a debate nor full-fledged "theology." It is, rather, a tip of the iceberg exercise in which together you surface the characteristics which would distinguish such a parish. Do it with newsprint. Ask parishioners to tell you how in their view and experience they would identify a spiritually successful contemporary American parish. There are no rights or wrongs. And, again, no debate. If differences of opinion emerge, simply ask for a show of hands as to whether the moot item should or should not be included in your "idealized design." If the majority say yes, include it; if not, discard it. In the end, while admittedly in a sketchy and incomplete fashion, you will all have set up a sort of model of the way you would prefer your own parish to be.

2. ACCOUNTABILITY PROFILE

    To be effective, your plan must specify accountabilities, i.e., who is to do what how in what time-frame. You cannot do this properly unless and until you know specifically who now does what how in your parish. In short you must develop early on an accountability profile. Using a common form, ask each person and group now active in your name to detail what he/she/it does. At the same time, on the same form, ask him/her/it to indicate future objectives in the subject area with which he/she/it is concerned. Existing "job descriptions" should be included in the returned data. In this way you accomplish two things: first, you have a current record of what is being done by whom how; second, you profit from objective suggestions from people now involved as to how you should proceed toward future objectives in your plan.

3. WIDER WE

    When you have completed *REDISCOVERY*, summarize your data in each of the three categories. Edit and gather it in a double-spaced, clear, and clean booklet. Circulate it widely, e.g., a copy to everyone at your weekend Masses. Do likewise with the data you derive in ENGAGEMENT. This will stimulate participation in COMMITMENT. Even those who do not participate will have been informed.

4. EVALUATION/UPDATE

(See following pages.) Plans are marching orders, not a terminal parade! One consultant tells his clients when they have done a plan, "fine, now we can begin." Your goals will, hopefully, be accomplished in three years, your objectives in one. Likewise, if the demographics and/or fiscal state of your parish change appreciably, you may want to revisit your mission statement every five years.

5. ASSISTANCE

You may want to call on a member of your parish who is expert in "planagement" to facilitate and guide you. Make sure, though, you all use the same language. (See glossary.) Otherwise you risk having a Tower of Babel. You should also find help from your diocesan councils and/or planning office. In smaller and simpler parishes, perhaps you can go it alone. In larger and/or more complex parishes, it is wise to summon this kind of assistance as your council plans.

6. DEMOCRACY OF MEANS

Many parish councils get hung up on the advisory versus decisive dilemma. A good parish plan ends this dilemma! Here's how it works. Once a council has developed a plan and the pastor has approved it, then a kind of democracy of means is enabled in which the council is decisive. Ends (goals) have been agreed and proclaimed. It becomes the task of the council to decide how best these ends can be attained (objectives). There are two conditions— first, that the council does not exceed the resource capacity of its parish (e.g., available dollars); second, that the council works within the parameters of universal, diocesan, and local Church directives. For instance, if a goal is to double the regular enrollment in high school CCD classes, then the council, within the two conditions, deliberates and decides how best this can be done year

Sharing/Planning

by goal year. Clearly, this sort of democracy of means is one of the principal benefits of a good parish plan!

[1] Archbishop John Roach to the Archdiocesan Assembly, St. Paul, Minn., April 24, 1976.
[2] John Dreher, Diocese of Providence, 1979.
[3] Arthur C. Beck, Jr., *Effective Decision Making For Parish Leaders* (Mystic, Conn.: XXIII Publications, 1973) 12.
[4] Earnest Larsen, *Spiritual Renewal of the American Parish* (Liguori, Mo.: Liguori Publications, 1975) 14.
[5] Ibid., 58.
[6] Felix M. Lopez, *Goal Setting Manual* (New York: Port Washington, 1974) 38.
[7] Gunnar Myrdal, cited in Ewald, *Environment and Change* (Bloomington, Ind.: Indiana University Press, 1968) 252.
[8] "To Teach as Jesus Did" (Washington: 1972) 138.

CHAPTER FIVE
EVALUATION

Putting all programs and activities regularly on trial for their lives and getting rid of those that cannot prove their productivity work wonders in stimulating creativity.[1]
What makes (control in any planning process) work is a system of following up—checking on the agreed date to see that an assignment has been completed.[2]

I. INSIGHT

Evaluation is measurement with an agreed ruler. Evaluation rates effectiveness, i.e., it appraises both performance and satisfaction. Evaluation:

- judges how effective an accountable person or group has been;
- in the accomplishment of the objective(s) for which the person or group has accepted accountability;
- in the agreed manner and within the agreed timespan.

Evaluation responds systematically to former Mayor Ed Koch's perennial question—"How'm I doing?" Evaluation is, thus, an indispensable element in any good planning process. If we don't measure our movement, if we simply proclaim horizons and then never check up to see how near we approach them, we cannot wisely decide what our future movements should be.

To evaluate a parish is to see how close it has in fact come to doing and becoming those things it said it would do and become. As the overall advisory body in its parish, the council is particularly charged to enable and administer periodic evaluations. Enumerating "several . . . functions that most parish councils undertake" one observer said:

> (Councils are) evaluators of the overall parish and various programs from the perspective of "the person in the pew."[3]

In its "Action Plan Manual: 1985-1990" the Diocese of Youngstown called for "an evaluation process (to) be built into the annual (parish) plan."[4] Earlier, the Diocese of San Diego did likewise:

PARISH EVALUATION

There is no effective uniform process for evaluating parishes on a regular basis that allows for the participation of the priest, the diocese, and the laity.

POLICY 61
There should be an evaluation of the parish on an annual basis by the Parish Council.

---

1. Evaluation should assist a parish in establishing specific goals and objectives to be accomplished within a specific evaluation period.
2. The priest self-evaluation should be an integral part of the parish evaluation. The self-evaluation, being a part of the parish evaluation, will help the priest to assess how he is fulfilling the parish needs and desires as well as his own goals and expectations during his assignment.[5]

In short, to plan well necessarily premises to evaluate well periodically!

Evaluation 43

But, in churches as elsewhere, evaluation is never easy, never simple. It can be "threatening" when its method and use are ambiguous. It can be spasmodic, superficial, only internal (i.e., self-evaluation period), inconsequential, etc. To be done positively, properly, and usefully, evaluation requires:

1. that its rationale, its norms, and its process (e.g., papers, schedules, report dates), be clear, understood, and agreed all around, i.e., by both evaluators and evaluatees, beforehand;
2. that its benefits must in fact and in perception outweigh its cost in time, paperwork, meetings, probable stress, both for the parish and for those who are to be evaluated;
3. that there be no exceptions, i.e., that all persons and groups who advise in the parish must be included. (This does not, of course, rule out the occasional need for particular evaluations in a moment of transition or crisis);
4. that there be a clear and agreed statement of what will be done with evaluation findings by whom and how;
5. that somehow so far as feasible a "customer" and a "peer" critique of the evaluated persons and groups be woven into the process, thus extending it beyond mere self-appraisals.

The only people in a position to evaluate the supportive nature of the church organization are the members not the leaders.[6]

Once again, self-judgments alone cannot suffice. There is always an urgency when we evaluate a person or group somehow to do a market analysis. How is this person or group perceived and experienced by those he/she/it serves?

Already thirty years ago, McGregor's Theory Y of management proposed that people want to and can be better motivated than forced to do things. Put another way, one critic defines effective management as:

> Guiding human and physical resources into dynamic organization units which attain their objectives to the satisfaction of those served and with a high degree of morale and sense of attainment on the part of those rendering the service.[7]

44 *Evaluation*

Still another writes:

> We will have to satisfy both the objective needs . . . for performance by the organization and the needs of the person for achievement and fulfillment.[8]

To sum up, parish evaluation must:
   a. be comprehensive at least periodically;
   b. measure both performance and satisfaction;
   c. involve, at least periodically, a kind of market analysis through which evaluatee "customers" and "peers" are canvased. (This in furtherance of the wisdom in Henry Ford's dictum:

> I find out what the customers want. I give it to them and I follow up with excellent after-sales service.)[9]

II. IMPACT

How does a parish council evaluate? First of all, it examines and fulfills the criteria listed on page XX. This peaks in a meeting with all evaluators and evaluatees in which the local process is specifically dialogued and detailed.

Self-evaluation.

Each group to be evaluated and each person is asked to complete the following form and return it to the council by a given date. (Note: while the sample form herewith is set up for group evaluation, by changing pronouns it can be similarly used for evaluatee persons.)

Self-Evaluation Report

Group: _____
Person Submitting: _____
Title:_____ Date:_____

1. These, briefly, were our objectives in the *past* work year. (In each instance, check your accomplishment record in the subject area.)

	Accomplished		Not
	Fully	Partly*	Accomplished*
Obj. #1_____	☐	☐	☐
Obj. #2_____	☐	☐	☐
Obj. #3_____	☐	☐	☐

*Where some objective was only accomplished in part or was not accomplished, please list on the reverse the reasons which impeded the group—internal to it and/or external.

2. Our group objectives in the *next* work year are these. (If you as yet have not been given such objectives, please suggest what you feel they should be. Identify the latter with an S.)

   Obj. #1 _____
   Obj. #2 _____
   Obj. #3 _____

3. As a measure of your group sense of satisfaction, of self-fulfillment, please check as appropriate below.

	Agree Strongly	Agree	?	Disagree	Disagree Strongly
3.1 Our work is important.	☐	☐	☐	☐	☐
3.2 We see reasonable progress in our work.	☐	☐	☐	☐	☐
3.3 Our work is appreciated in our parish.	☐	☐	☐	☐	☐

46 *Evaluation*

4. Please add on the reverse or on attached sheet(s) any other comments which will help the parish council better to understand the effectiveness (performance + satisfaction) of your group.

But, again, self-evaluation is not sufficient. It must be complemented by a kind of "market analysis," i.e., an indication as to how the parish as a whole perceives and experiences the evaluated persons and groups. To do this, the following form is proposed.

External (Consumer) Evaluation Report

I am a priest □, staff person □, member of a parish council/committee/task force □.

I am a deacon □, sister □, layman □, laywoman □.

I have been in this parish for _____ years.

1. Overall, I judge our parish to be:
dynamic □, inertial □, active □, truly participatory □, mediocre □, losing ground □, other _____.
(More than one of the above may be checked.)

2. List here all evaluatee persons and groups in the parish.

	Serves Us Well	Serves Us Poorly	Other
e.g.			
2.1 Pastor	□	□	_____
2.2 Parish Staff	□	□	_____
2.3 Parish Council	□	□	_____
2.4 Liturgy Committee	□	□	_____
etc.			

3. These are the STRENGTHS of our parish.

_____

_____

_____

4. These are the areas in which our parish needs to IMPROVE.

_____

_____

5. Please add on the reverse or on attached sheet(s) any other thoughts which can help us evaluate ourselves better and grow better together in "grace and wisdom."

Once you have gathered the completed forms, convene your council and review what they tell you. In most instances, you will have simply gathered helpful data. This in itself is of maximum importance as you plan ahead. In some instances, you will find what I describe as *red flags*. There is indication in the self-evaluations and/or in the external evaluations that something needs to be done to assist evaluated persons or groups to improve. Here, further contact and analysis is urgent. Again, though, you intervene in such cases not to punish or accuse but rather to help the red flagged person and/or group to do a better job for and with all of you!

[1] Peter F. Drucker, *The Effective Executive* (New York: Harper, 1966) 108.
[2] Williams, *Improving Parish Management*, 45.
[3] Robert R. Newsome, *The Ministering Parish* (Ramsey, N.J.: Paulist Press, 1982) 78.

[4] "Action Plan Manual: 1985-1990," 61.
[5] Synod II, San Diego, Cal., March 1976, 83-84.
[6] Waynich, to the National Pastoral Planning Convention.
[7] Lawrence A. Appley, *Formula for Success* (New York: American Management Association, 1974) 13.
[8] Drucker, *The Effective Executive*, 173.
[9] Cited in Heller, *The Super Managers* (New York: Dutton, 1984) 194.

CHAPTER SIX
PROCEDURE

I. INSIGHT

Many council constitutions and by laws call for the use of Robert's Rules in council proceedings, e.g., Baltimore (1973), La Crosse (1980). Others call for "consensus." The debate continues. Robert's Rules moves through motion, discussion, and vote. Consensus moves toward agreement otherwise than through formal votes.

The case for consensus has been put thus:

> In the collegial style of the church inherent in the documents of Vatican II, it seems better for parish councils . . . to try to arrive at most decisions through consensus.[1]

The critic in this case admits that "there is a place for both methods (consensus and Robert's Rules) in decision-making,"[2] but suggests that "voting is adequate for minor matters and consensus is good for major matters."[3] The principal arguments for "consensus" are that it is not "competitive" and produces "no winners and losers"[4] and that Robert's Rules are "legalistic" and tend to result in "bogged down" meetings.

The arguments for Robert's Rules, on the other hand, are several. First, that this is the procedure to which most Americans are accustomed and feel at home with. Second, that this surfaces specific action ideas on which majority/minority sentiments are recorded. Third, that while consensus is included in this method, consensus does not in turn include Robert's

49

Rules. Arguing against "consensus," advocates of Robert's Rules contend: a) it frequently results in amorphous, even platitudinous recommendations; b) it is subject to much manipulation, e.g., by determined small groups; c) it does not leave what might be called a tangible, actionable residue, i.e., clear and clean resolutions; and/or d) it intrudes on the conscience of participants who are not offered the chance for a secret written ballot. Proponents of Robert's Rules likewise argue that there are "winners" and "losers" also in "consensus." Deciders lose because they are not provided with specific action proposals and because they cannot be sure how many agreed out of "social pressure" rather than through conviction. Participants may lose because of "social pressure" from voluble advocates. The council itself can lose from a turn off of possible members who come to perceive it as merely a "discussion group," quite unlike any similar civic, business, or fraternal body to which they belong and which uses Robert's Rules.

I am well aware that many ecclesial persons now canonize "consensus." And I concede that perhaps, where it is expertly practised, many of the objections proposed in the above paragraph may be overcome. We are, however, dealing with a largely amateur practice, and here my wide experience tells me most of the objections are not infrequently valid. It should be noted here again that there is nothing in Vatican II, in the Code of Canon Law, or anywhere else officially which requires the use of either method in council procedure! And yet I suspect, though they may be circumspect and subliminal in their semantics, there are not a few council advisors who at least imply some sort of magisterial imperative for "consensus." My own preference is for *a judicious admixture* of the two methods. I would, however, reverse the order suggested by the critic above. In my view, "consensus" should be used by a council when dealing with relatively minor, non-controversial agenda items, Robert's Rules otherwise.

II. IMPACT

This matter should not be left to chance. It should be clearly spelled out in council by laws. This can be done in several ways. One way is by specifying that certain items, e.g., personnel, finance, goal formulation, should be decided by the council using Robert's Rules, i.e., by motion, full discussion, and written ballot. In all other instances "consensus" shall be used. Another way is by establishing "consensus" as the "normal" council procedure, but providing that the president, the executive committee, and/or any four or five members may ask that Robert's Rules be used on any particular item. A third way, and probably the best of all, is by combining one and two.

In any case, whatever method is used, there must be from and for every council *a tangible residue*. I mean by this written and numbered recommendations, whether arrived at by "consensus" or by Robert's Rules. If, on the other hand, a council does nothing but brainstorm with no visible and traceable outcomes, it will quickly be perceived as only a think tank with no clout and no consequence. These tangible residues, recommendations, should be reported in boxes which stand out from single spaced "minutes" and tabulated annually, and the council should be told at the end of each work year what in fact happened to each proposal. In this way the amorphous and sometimes platitudinous common-denominatoring which afflicts at least many practices of disembodied "consensus" is avoided.

EXAMPLE

> Recommendation 1990, 1: That a three-day retreat be enabled and implemented in St. Robert Parish prior to the end of this work year.

52 Procedure

[1] Williams, *Improving Parish Management*, 60.
[2] Ibid.
[3] Ibid.
[4] Ibid.

CHAPTER SEVEN
PASTORAL ASSEMBLY/TASK FORCES

I. INSIGHT

Not infrequently in this booklet, the words WIDER WE surface. The expression was coined by the then Bishop of Saginaw Francis E. Reh in the mid-1970s. Serving in the diocese at that time, I have since co-opted it. It means that, if we really intend to practice what we preach about "shared responsibility," there is an urgency to extend continually both the *quantity* of those who share and the *quality* of their sharing! It is also a challenging expression of the "planagement" principle that the more people *own* and honestly participate in the process through which decisions are made which affect them, the more likely it is that they will effectively carry out those decisions.

Each parish council, however good, is necessarily few in numbers. It is, thus, imperative that opportunities for an ever WIDER WE to "become part of the process" be regularly provided. There are several ways, two in particular.

I.1 *Pastoral Assembly*

This is an annual gathering of the parish to which all are invited and which is strongly promoted. Admittedly, not all will come. But the numbers should far exceed those who are attracted by an "open" meeting of the council. Admittedly, the "kooks" will come "out of the wall." But the common sense of the parish as a whole will overwhelm their eccentricity. And better to expose them than to let them fester in the plaster! Admittedly, it is increasingly difficult to get people "to turn out." But at least an assembly with substance and "clout," and again strongly promoted, should be widely attended.

A good assembly provides these benefits to a parish, its pastor, and its council:

1. It is a sign of unity and commonwealth;
2. It may well surface new leadership persons;
3. It identifies a regular "consumer" profile and is an excellent chance to "poll the parish";
4. It challenges all parish groups and persons to "stand up and be counted," i.e., to report to and take guidance from a large number of ordinary parishioners;
5. It exemplifies and enables a WIDER WE;
6. It is an excellent "communications" vehicle.

In a 1988 survey of parish council guidelines in thirteen (arch)dioceses, six provided for just such an assembly.

I.2 Task Forces

It is abundantly evident that most Americans simply will not accept membership of what I call eternal committees either in Church or in state. (An eternal committee is, for instance, a committee that meets the third Thursday evening in each work month forever.) This is also true of the parochial We. But each parishioner has graces and talents. Even if he/she will not become a committee member, opportunities for involvement must be provided. One way is through the annual pastoral assembly, another is through task forces enabled by the council.

A task force is given a specific task and a specific timeline. Once it has done its task, it disbands. I am convinced more Catholics will respond to such limited challenges than currently respond to the challenge of eternal committees.

II. IMPACT

A *pastoral assembly* should:
  a. be administered by the council;
  b. be very widely preached and promoted;
  c. be an annual event, either at the start or end of each work year;
  d. be provided with written as well as oral reports;
  e. be prospective as well as retrospective.

A simple notice on the parochial bulletin board will not suffice as promotion! Telephone brigades are urgent, repeated emphases, PR in the news media, a covered dish meal. The purpose of an assembly is to hear the pastor-in-council and to guide the pastor-in-council as the parish plans ahead. There are many ways to structure such an assembly. Here is one:

Pastoral Assembly—St. Robert Parish USA
Saturday

9:00 AM Registration. Coffee, juice, rolls.
9:30 AM Convening prayer.
9:45 AM Welcome. Agenda/logistics detail.
10:00 AM Remarks—pastor, council. (These to have been summarized, reproduced, and distributed to all participants.)
Survey forms distributed if survey appropriate.
10:30 AM Small group discussion.
11:15 AM Plenary session to evaluate past/present.
Noon   Lunch.

TODAY

56 Pastoral Assembly/Task Forces

		T
1:00 PM	Remarks—pastor, council. (These to have been summarized, reproduced, and distributed to all participants.)	O M O
1:30 PM	Small group discussion.	R
2:30 PM	Report from small groups (fish bowl).	R O
3:15 PM	Plenary session to evaluate future thrusts and recommend directions. Survey forms returned.	W
4:00 PM	Assembly Mass.	

Task forces. Each task force should:

a. be chaired by a council member;
b. include relevant non council members;
c. be connected, as appropriate, to a council committee;
d. be given a written commission;
e. be assigned specific report back date(s).

Here is an example of how this can be done:

Assembly Task Force—St. Robert Parish USA

TASK:	To organize as primary facilitators and to publicize our annual parish pastoral assembly—June 9, 1991.
CHAIR:	Co-Chairs (council members) Mary Doe, John Smith.
MEMBERS:	(here list others members.)
START DATE:	January 15, 1991
REPORT DATES:	1. To report by April 1, 1991 on progress to date—to pastor and council executive committee; 2. To report by May 1, 1991 on subsequent progress, etc., to pastor and plenary council—in writing; 3. To evaluate assembly and report to pastor and council executive committee by July 1, 1991—in writing.
DISBAND DATE:	July 2, 1991

CHAPTER EIGHT
PASTOR AND COUNCIL

A good king is one whose subjects prosper.
—*an old folk saying*

I. INSIGHT

In official documentation, e.g., the papers of Vatican II and the Code of Canon Law, no specific norms are provided for the pastor-council interface. In *The Directory on the Pastoral Ministry of Bishops*, however, certain guidelines are enunciated in regard to the diocesan pastoral council. It seems reasonable to assume that parallel considerations apply in a parish. Here are relevant citations from the Directory, emphasis supplied:

1. By its reflection the council furnishes the judgments necessary to enable the diocesan community to *plan* its pastoral program *systematically and to fulfill* it *effectively;*[1]

2. The council has only a *consultative* voice; nevertheless the bishop has *great respect* for its recommendations for they offer his apostolic office the *serious and settled cooperation of the ecclesiastical community;*[2]

3. In order that the council may actually achieve this goal, it will be helpful if *study* precedes their common deliberations; and, if the case warrants, the help of *institutes or offices that work in the field may be used;*[3]

4. (Among "general norms referring specifically to pastoral cooperation") the *plan of action* must first be *collegially* drawn up in writing;[4]

5. In place of hindrance, discord, and confusion there should be rather a feeling of a *common responsibility* with everyone working together to achieve one and the same goal.[5]

Likewise, it seems reasonable to draw a parochial parallel from the Vatican's Circular Letter on diocesan councils (January 31, 1973). This document confirms to these councils accountability in a very wide range of pastoral concerns. Earlier, in his Motu Proprio *Ecclesiae Sanctae* (August 1966) Paul VI charged diocesan councils with specific responsibility in preparing for and monitoring the implementation of synods.

Beyond these guiding ideas, we can perhaps best place the role of a pastor vis-à-vis his parish councils by looking at some recent "guidelines":

1. The Dogmatic Constitution on the Church asks pastors to "recognize and promote the dignity as well as the responsibility of the layman in the Church." Let them willingly make use of his prudent advice.[6]

   A pastor establishes a council to expand and enhance the decision-making process of 1) pastoral planning and goal-setting, 2) developing and implementing pastoral programs, 3) improving pastoral services, 4) evaluating pastoral effectiveness.[7]

   The priest as a builder of community is a unifier, coordinator, and mediator within the council . . . The priest helps the council to realize its responsibilities through an understanding of Church teaching, Code of Canon Law, and archdiocesan policy.[8]

   One of the most important ways that a pastor shows respect for the talents and abilities of parishioners is by involving them in the activities and planning of the parish.[9]

2. Lay people who are outstanding in the requisite knowledge, prudence, and integrity, are capable of being experts and advisors (citing Canon 228, 2). (Nevertheless) only the pastor is responsible for and has to answer to the bishop or parish community for the decisions taken, even though these have been developed and taken together with others.[10]

3. To carry out effectively their heavy responsibility pastors really need the encouragement of the people, and people really need the encouragement of their pastors. The clergy need to learn from the people, and the people need to learn from their clergy.[11]

4. The communal style encouraged by the parish council allows the priest to share his human feelings and also to gain knowledge from the wisdom and experience of other council members. The council's pursuit of true Christianity can lead the priest to a deeper life of prayer and a clearer understanding of his role as spiritual leader.[12]

5. The pastor should provide opportunities for the council to grow spiritually . . . (Also) outside help for the continued training of members or for the better facilitation of council meetings.[13]

A pastoral council is meant to be a way for the pastor to come to know even more intensely the feelings of his parishioners and a way for parishioners to exercise responsibility for the life of the Church.[14]

From such citations as these a profile of the pastor-council relationship emerges. The pastor unifies, assists in spiritual growth, greatly respects, probes for a better awareness of parishioner actualities, involves his council in planning, etc. The council in turn, acknowledging the pastor's ultimate accountability, offers him the "serious and settled cooperation of the ecclesiastical community," continuously respiritualizes and reinforms itself, is rightly concerned with all pastoral activities, is the primary planning committee in its parish, etc.

As it does these things, it becomes companion to its pastor as the active custodian and enabler of the principle of pastoral wholeness vis-à-vis those persons and groups operating within a parallel principle of judicious subsidiarity.

II. IMPACT

This entire text is designed to resource constellar councils, i.e., councils in which relationships are overt and systemic. The pastor-council interface is such a relationship. It is, thus, not necessary to do more here than to suggest certain brief additional action ideas:

1. A good council recognizes the *hierarchic authority* of its pastor. One set of guidelines puts it this way:

   > Priests are servants of the collegial process that should distinguish a parish council . . . (They are) brothers among brothers . . . neither authoritative dictators nor powerless symbols.[15]

   A good pastor recognizes and has "great respect" for his council. Should he, for instance, be constrained to negate one of its recommendations, he responds promptly indicating his reasons in writing and, wherever possible, proposing an alternative way to handle the matter in question.

2. A good council is carefully, currently, and comprehensively *informed* by its pastor (and staff) both as to the "state of souls" and "the temporalities" in the parish so that it can responsibly respond to them.

3. A good pastor and a good council will acknowledge a continuing need for authentic *"spiritual discernment."* They will witness to each other again and again. They will engage in moments of mutual recollection and retreat. They will ponder together and plan for "the state of souls" as well as "the temporalities" of the parish they share.

A successful council will have regular opportunities for prayerful reflection and regular reminders to its members to seek and to do the will of God.[16]

4. A good pastor will face up to the fact that even the best council is few in numbers. He will challenge and assist the council to involve an ever WIDER parochial WE in a kind of common "ownership of the parish," this, for example, through an annual pastoral *assembly* and through the repeated use of *task forces* rather than eternal committees.

5. A good pastor and a good council will know that:

   The success of a parish council will depend on the strength of the *relationships*.[17]

   Pastors will work with councils to promote system and to energize working coherences. Put another way, dangling participles make no more sense in an ecclesial institution than they do anywhere else! Still another metaphor suggests that the job of any leader is to show his or her followers where their common north is. Surely the same can be said of a council and its pastor. The Master is, of course, our North! But it remains the accountability of pastors-in-councils to translate this high bench mark into practical directions in the parishes they serve. The best way I know to do this consistently and coherently is through a good parish pastoral plan in the preparation and implementation of which pastor and council pray and act together. Likewise, through annual pastoral assemblies, plan directions are reviewed, evaluated, and further advanced. We come back as we started to the mandate of Vatican II: "a common effort to attain fullness in unity."[18]

6. A good pastor will recognize that *Americans will not meet to meet. They will meet only when there is red meat on the agenda table!* Some wag once suggested that the practice of parish councils let the laity in on a secret. Running a par-

ish is not all tunes of glory. By the law of averages, much of a council's gathering time must be focused in on relatively uninspiring detail. Still, unless and until there are substantial items frequently in its diet, what I call red meat, a council will die of anemia. True, some parishioners will assemble whatever the agenda. But if we honestly want to involve and commit an ever WIDER parochial WE, councils must deal with major matters often. A council which plays only Trivial Pursuit soon withers away into inconsequence! Likewise, if and as a council is in fact segregated away from major matters of pastoral concern. For example, if a council is told "don't touch education; we have a committee for this. Don't touch liturgy; we have a committee for that," etc., who in his or her right mind would want to serve on such a council?

Once in a parish in Bay City, Michigan, I moderated an open goal session. When the session was over, I sat with the pastor in his rectory. He allowed as to how the meeting had been "interesting." But, he continued, "they didn't tell me anything I didn't already know!" My response was quick and brief. *Dabitur vobis?* "That's just it, Father," I said, "they told you." For the first time in that good parish some one hundred people had turned out and come up with, presumably, much the same corporate vision their good pastor had already developed. Far from intruding on or competing with the pastor, they had significantly enlarged his support base. They may, even, have added a few new dimensions. As he reached toward a better parochial future, he could now count on a core of shared vision and cooperation which had not before been overt. This sort of thing, I suggest, is a paramount outcome when good pastors honestly and enthusiastically work with good councils—and vice versa!

[1] *The Directory on the Pastoral Ministry of Bishops* (Vatican City: 1973) par. 204.
[2] Ibid.
[3] Ibid.
[4] Ibid., par. 209a.
[5] Ibid., par. 209b.
[6] *The Parish Pastoral Council* (Canadian Conference of Catholic Bishops: 1984) 37.
[7] John R. Keating, *A Pastoral Letter on Consultation in the Parish* (Arlington, VA.: 1984) 18.
[8] *Guidelines for the Ministry of Parish Councils* (Archdiocese of St. Louis: 1985) 16.
[9] *Guidelines for Parish Councils* (Diocese of Rockville Centre: 1987) 6.
[10] *The Parish Pastoral Council*, 16.
[11] Keating, *A Pastoral Letter*, 9.
[12] *Guidelines for the Ministry*, 16.
[13] *Guidelines for Parish Councils*, 6.
[14] Ibid., 8.
[15] Bernard M. Harcarik, *Spiritual Renewal Through Structural Reform* (Diocese of Pittsburgh, 1975) 20.
[16] Williams, *Improving Parish Management*, 77.
[17] Harcarik, *Spiritual Renewal*, 33.
[18] Vatican II, Church, 13.

CHAPTER NINE
CHECK LIST FOR YOUR PARISH COUNCIL

1. Are we a prayer group as well as a planning group? Has membership of this council inspirited us and the parish we serve? *Or* do we settle for perfunctory "invocations" and/or seldom gather apart to reflect on and replenish our spiritual mission?
2. Do we partner well as a kind of lead star in a parochial constellation? Are we actively related to other parish boards and committees? *Or* are we just another light in a parochial Milky Way in which, whatever the "book" says, there is little system?
3. Have we developed or are we developing an effective parish plan? Are we working toward agreed horizons? *Or* do we simply drift from crisis to crisis, with no overall itinerary and reference point?
4. Are we in fact growing "in grace and wisdom?" *Or* are we content to hold the parochial fort in a kind of "static goodness?"
5. Are we tackling the really big opportunities and problems in our parish? *Or* do we dodge major issues and play Trivial Pursuit?
6. Do we provide chances for parishioners who are not members of our council or of other parochial groups to share

their graces and talents with us? Do we, for example, administer annual assemblies and task forces thus enabling an ever WIDER parochial WE? *Or* is participation in our parish limited to serving on some eternal committee?

7. Do we regularly evaluate the persons and groups, including ourselves, who represent us? Do we estimate the facts and feelings in our yesterday and today before we plan ahead to our corporate tomorrow? *Or* do we fail to judge the past and the present in an uninformed rush to our future?

8. Do we operate like an island? Do we factor into our attitudes and goals our situation as a benefiting and contributing member of two larger communities—one ecclesial, the other civil? *Or* are we ostriches with our heads buried in only local sand?

9. Are we enthusiastic in and open to the Spirit like they were at the first Pentecost? *Or* are we bland, lukewarm, uninspired and uninspiring? "I came to put fire on earth," said the Master. Are we rather half-life embers?

10. Are there tangible residues from our meetings, specific recommendations which can be tracked, results? *Or* do we merely brainstorm, dialoguing but seldom consequential?

METHODOLOGY

A. Ask each member of your council to respond to each of the above questions. Use the rating system you prefer, e.g.

      GOOD   FAIR   POOR   OTHER

or

      1 (best state)   2   3   4   5 (worst state)

B. Gather the responses and cumulate them.

Check List for Your Parish Council

C. Identify those question areas in which the cumulative response is largely negative.
D. Engage in collective "spiritual discernment."

FEED THROUGH

E. Complete the following matrix:

AREA IN WHICH WE NEED TO IMPROVE	IMPROVEMENT ACTION	
	Next Work Year	Subsequently
e.g. Evaluation (Q #7)	Dialogue, design, and communicate an evaluation process and papers.	In the second work year, implement. In the third work year, review and judge the process and papers, then redesign as appropriate.

F. ACT

CHAPTER TEN
MODEL CONSTITUTION AND BYLAWS

It is sometimes contended that providing a council with a formal constitution and bylaws suggests too great a parallel with civic and business "boards." Better to work loosely responding to the "surprises of the Spirit" and avoiding procedural strait jackets! On the other hand, when people gather in any regular working association there must at least be agreed and explicit norms to guide them. True, there were no constitutional details at Pentecost. But there were none also at the Tower of Babel. And, as the captain of any crew will attest, where there are many rowers there is always a need for stroke patterns.

In short, if a council is to be truly and consistently effective, constitutional questions must be answered beforehand.

What follows is a kind of model set of constitutional articles and bylaws. They incorporate the ideas enunciated in this text. Again, I cannot in one overall norm accommodate every local situation and preference. I am well aware that differences of opinion may exist. And the arguments on the other side will be often persuasive. Still, better to provide a model than to leave such ideas loose-ended! Adjustment to particular councils can and will be made by my readers.

St. Robert Parish   Crossroads, USA

PARISH PASTORAL COUNCIL
Constitution and Bylaws

Article I: Definition

The name of this organization shall be the St. Robert Parish Council speaking for and in the name of the people of God of this parish.

BYLAW

A parishioner is a person who a) has been baptized and is in communion with the Roman Catholic Church, and either b) lives within the official boundaries of St. Robert Parish or c) by his or her free and consistent choice wants to be a member of St. Robert Parish and contributes to the betterment of this parochial community of faith, grace, and service.

Article II: Mission

The purpose of this Council is to constitute the primary consultative voice of the people of God in St. Robert Parish as that people shares responsibility with its pastor and staff, offering them what the Vatican describes as "the serious and settled cooperation of the ecclesiastical community."

BYLAW

Once it is constituted, the Council shall pray, dialogue, and develop its own particular mission statement stressing the spiritual rationale for its existence. This statement shall be reviewed and, as appropriate, reaffirmed or updated every five (5) years.

Article III: Membership

The Council shall encompass fifteen (15) members. Not more than five (5) shall be ex officio and/or appointed. Members shall serve a three (3) year term and be eligible for one (1) immediately consecutive term.

BYLAW

The parish as a whole shall periodically elect ten (10) members, staggering the terms so that there is an annual turnover of not less than three (3) elected members. Ex officio members shall include the pastor and the DRE. Three (3) members may be appointed by the pastor, to provide additional representations and/or competences, with the advice and consent of the Council.

Article IV: Officers and Executive Committee

The pastor or his delegate shall preside at each Council meeting. The Council shall annually elect one (1) of its elected members as Chair, one (1) of its members as Vice Chair and one (1) of its members as Secretary. The Executive Committee shall encompass the three (3) officers plus the chairs of the two (2) Council standing committees.

BYLAW

Officers shall serve one (1) year terms and be eligible for election to not more than two (2) immediately consecutive one (1) year terms.

Article V: Meetings

The Council shall normally meet every other month in each work year.

BYLAW

Annually, the normal meeting schedule shall be agreed and announced at the first meeting in each work year. At least one (1) such meeting annually shall be overnight. One purpose of this meeting is to enable a mini-retreat. Special Council meetings may be called by a) the pastor, b) the executive committee, pastor agreeing, and/or c) a written request signed by not less than four (4) members of the Council. At least ten (10) days advance notice shall be given all members of such special meetings.

Article VI: Standing Committees and Task Forces

The Council shall have two (2) standing committees—a Pastoral Planning Committee and an Administration and Finance Committee. Normally and as appropriate, these committees shall convene in those months when the Council does not meet in plenary session. Otherwise, the Council shall work through task forces.

BYLAW

The Pastoral Planning Committee shall, if one does not already exist, pray, dialogue, and develop an effective parish pastoral plan. It shall administer the annual parish pastoral assembly. It shall periodically evaluate progress toward agreed parish goals and objectives and update the plan. The Administration and Finance Committee shall speak for and to the Council on matters of administration, maintenance, etc., and shall be in St. Robert Parish the finance council called for in the Code of Canon Law.

Task forces shall be appointed by the Council as appropriate. Each task force shall be given a) a written commission and b) a specific timeline in which its work is to be completed.

Members of Standing Committees and task forces need not be simultaneously Council members but each shall be chaired by a Council member.

(It is here assumed that other appropriate committees exist in the parish, e.g., liturgy, schools. Such committees may or may not be simultaneously formal committees of the council. In either case, they operate with considerable autonomy [subsidiarity]. It remains, however, urgent that the council be made continuously aware of their activities and recommendations. This, again, in furtherance of the principle of pastoral wholeness and in avoidance of the Milky Way parish syndrome. Where a plan exists, the council's charge is to monitor and evaluate implementation of that plan via its own and companion committees. Once more, no major area of pastoral concern should be segregated away from a council's right and obligation to overview it.)

Article VII: Procedure

Normally the Council and its committees and task forces shall proceed using the method known as consensus. In particular instances, however, it shall proceed using the method known as Robert's Rules. Such instances shall include, but not be restricted to, matters of finance and personnel. The members present at a Council meeting shall constitute a quorum.

Model Constitution and Bylaws 71

BYLAW

Normally, the Council will pray, dialogue, and come to resolution on agenda items without a formal vote, i.e., seeking consensus among its members. Robert's Rules may, however, be invoked by a) the pastor, b) the executive committee, and/or c) any four (4) members of the Council. This may occur when the agenda item is highly controversial, when a written record of Council opinion is deemed appropriate, and/or when the item suggests that members vote more free from "social pressure" in a written ballot than *viva voce*, on matters of personnel and finance, etc. The request for use of Robert's Rules shall be non-debatable.

Whatever process is employed, or whatever combination of methods, each Council recommendation shall be a) numbered annually and b) reported in a separate box standing out from the minutes. Progress on all such recommendations in a specific work year shall be reported back to the Council in writing by the executive committee at the final meeting in that work year.

Article VIII: Pastoral Planning

Pastoral planning is a principal function of this Council.

BYLAW

With its Pastoral Planning and its Administration and Finance Committees as its workhorses, the Council shall implement and evaluate progress under the existing parish pastoral plan and/or proceed promptly to pray, dialogue, and develop a plan. Pastoral planning encompasses both such matters as goal-setting, accountability, relationships, and those events, groups, and processes through which an ever WIDER WE shares responsibility in St. Robert Parish.

Article IX: Assembly

With its Pastoral Planning Committee as its implementing agent, the Council shall administer an annual pastoral assembly in St. Robert Parish.

BYLAW

All parishioners are summoned to this annual event which dialogues parish "mission" and "business." The Council shall report in writing to the assembly, i.e., its track record, its tentatives, its prospect. The Council shall take appropriate guidance from the assembly as its plans ahead.

Article X: Amendment/Appeal

This constitution and accompanying bylaws may be amended by the Council. Non-accepted Council recommendations may be resubmitted.

BYLAW

For amendment, a two-thirds vote of the Council at any meeting, pastor agreeing, and notice of such proposed amendment in writing at the meeting prior to such vote are required.

In the event of non-acceptance of a Council recommendation by the pastor, he shall notify the Council in writing of his reason(s), and the Council by a two-thirds vote may rethink, reword, and resubmit a similar recommendation. If this second recommendation is likewise not accepted by the pastor, the matter is terminated.

GLOSSARY

ACCOUNTABILITY: This is the process and the expectation and commitment through which a person or group agrees and is commissioned to accomplish a given task or set of tasks in a given manner by a given completion date. Accountability, thus, is highly specific. Accountabilities should be assigned to persons and groups that a) are willing to accept them, b) are capable of accomplishing them, and c) so far as possible are enthusiastic, even eager, to do them.

ASSEMBLY: A parish assembly is a periodic, usually annual, gathering of the members of a parish community. Open to all and strongly promoted in advance, its purpose is to advise the council, pastor, and staff on all matters of parochial mission and business significance. It reviews past activities. It recommends future actions. It does so in and through appropriate processes of spiritual discernment. Like the council with which it is fundamentally teamed, an assembly has "a consultative voice".

COMMITMENT: This is the third step in a parish planning process. Here, at a series of open meetings, the parish as a whole deliberates the REDISCOVERY data and the drafts from ENGAGEMENT, decides, and, as an ever WIDER WE, proposes a good pastoral plan.

CONSULTATIVE VOICE: These words in the Code of Canon Law and elsewhere indicate that the council and, by association the assembly and other parochial boards, recommends to the pastor in an advisory rather than a compelling dimension. He is not obliged to accept the recommendation. Considerations of prudence and mutual respect, however, dictate that, in the event a pastor negates such a recommendation, he should notify the originating body promptly, with his reasons for so doing in writing, and, whenever and wherever feasible, suggest alternative courses of action.

DEMOCRACY OF MEANS: Once a parish through its council, pastor, and staff, with such hierarchic approval as may be locally required, has agreed on and promulgated a parish pastoral plan, then through a democracy of means it becomes easily possible to avoid the debilitating "advisory-decisive" dilemma. With agreed an approved end states, i.e., goals and priorities, the council or other appropriate board decides the means of arriving at these end states. So long as a council a) is fiscally responsible and b) is loyal to Church teaching and orthodox practices, it is decisive not "merely advisory." Indeed, enablement of precisely such a democracy of means is a principal reason why pastoral plans are urgent in all parishes!

ECOLOGY: Ecology is the science of interrelationships, how each living organism impacts on and is in turn impacted by living organisms around it. There is *an ecology for parishes* too! No parish is an island. Every parish is a benefiting and contributing member of two larger communities. One of these is *ecclesial*. Parishes impact on and are in turn impacted by neighboring parishes—Catholic and non-Catholic. They also impact on and are in turn impacted by the deaneries, dioceses, and the Church Universal in which they locate. The other larger community is *civic*. Parishes impact on and are in turn impacted by the neighborhoods, towns/cities, etc., in which they locate. A parish council or plan which neglects this ecology is fundamentally flawed!

EFFECTIVENESS: Councils, parishes, and people are effective when they do good things better and when, in so doing, they feel more and more self-satisfied. Effectiveness = performance + satisfaction. A major reason why councils exist is to help their parishes become more effective.

ENGAGEMENT: This is the second step in a parish planning process. Here, with the data from REDISCOVERY in hand and much

Glossary 75

prayer, parish leaders convene and develop a *draft* mission statement plus germinal goals and objectives.

EVALUATION: This is the process through which, periodically, the accomplishment of or shortfall from an organization's plan, e.g., its goals and objectives, is explicitly measured in terms of actual performance, with subsequent changes in the plan or some of its accountabilities as appropriate.

GOAL: A goal is a relatively long-range target, usually with a timeline of three or five years. This target emerges from a previous mission statement. A goal begins with an action verb. A goal must not depend for accomplishment on a factor or factors over which the goal-setting organization has no control. As a whole goals must be consistent with one another and must not demand resources well beyond current organizational capacity. Each goal should be as measurable, as concrete, as possible. For example:

To improve our high school CCD is not a good goal.

To double the number of young people regularly participating in our high school CCD programs could, if it seems locally feasible, be a good goal.

Someone has aptly suggested that *goals are dreams with deadlines.* A goal, thus, is a kind of dream made feasible, timed, and specific. In my view, a better way to state this adage is: *goals are dreams with deadlines and lifelines!*

IDEALIZED DESIGN: This is a process through which members of an organization (e.g., parish), putting aside current resource constraints, consensus and record a systemic scenario for the organizational tomorrow they would prefer if they had all the necessary resources (dollars, people, facilities). This, in short, is their collective *dream.*

OBJECTIVE: An objective is a proposed program or set of related programs derivative from a previously agreed goal and with a one year timeline. Each objective must be a) measurable, b) costed in terms of the organization's resources (people, dollars, facilities), and c) assigned to accountable persons or groups ready, able, eager to do it. For example, an objective within the above model goal might be:

> To engage and to train three (3) couples in how to teach high school CCD well.

PARISH AS SYSTEM: Every parish, like every diocese, should be conceived and practiced as a whole or system composed basically of two subsystems or parts. One subsystem is operational, how the parish functions day by day. The second subsystem is consultative. It encompasses the processes and events through which people share responsibility in the parish. Both subsystems must overlap. The council must be continually alert to how the system is functioning and improve it as appropriate. Here is how the parochial system looks:

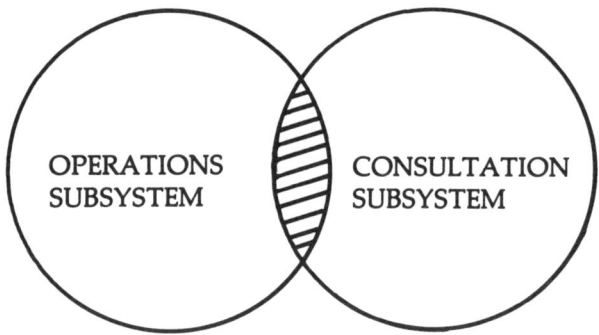

PASTORAL PLANNING: Pastoral planning is the systematic and widely participatory process through which a mission statement, goals, specific objectives, and accountabilities are dialogued, decided, and recorded in a plan which is periodically evaluated, reviewed, and as appropriate updated. No parish is an organization. Every parish has an organization. Pastoral planning seeks a) to make a parish more effective and b) in the process to involve an ever WIDER WE in parochial ownership. The council is the workhorse when a parish plans. (See also REDISCOVERY, ENGAGEMENT, COMMITMENT.)

REDISCOVERY: This is the first step in the parish pastoral planning process once the parish has decided to plan. It encompasses several elements:

i. an idealized design, i.e., a collective response to the question, what makes a spiritually successful contemporary American parish?
ii. how we *are*, i.e., the facts about ourselves such as finance, demography, the track record of the groups which represent us, etc.
iii. how we *feel*, i.e., a saturation survey on our strengths, areas in which we need to improve, and on specifics such as sermons, youth ministry, outreach, liturgy, etc.
iv. how we *partner*, i.e., how we locate as benefiting and contributing members of larger ecclesial and civic communities.

All this data, in each case current and comprehensive, is gathered clear and clean in a booklet which is then widely distributed in the parish.

RELATIONSHIP: It has often been suggested that the priesthood of today is fundamentally interactional. So too are all the elements in the contemporary parish. Indeed, a continual process of interaction is inescapable as both pastors and councils develop. Every parish and each of its leaders exist in an ecology. The science of ecology proposes that every living organism impacts on its surrounding organisms and is in turn impacted by them. Other words for this imperative characteristic are system and network. A parish council is inescapably situated in a series of two basic relationships. One of these is *horizontal*, i.e., with other parochial events, groups, and persons and with its neighbor churches and civic communities. The other is *vertical*, i.e., with its deanery, diocese, Church Universal, and ultimately with its Master. As it grows "in grace and wisdom," it must again and again factor in these fundamental relationships.

SYSTEM: A system is a whole composed of interacting parts. But systemic wholes are more than the mere sum of these individual parts or subsystems.

Notes